ABOUT BRADLEY TAYLOR

Bradley Taylor is an award-winning p(
Birmingham. He is the winner of the R

Bradley is the co-host and organiser of The Big Gay Poetry Night with fellow poet M. L. Walsh, which has featured poets such as Joelle Taylor, Kandace Siobhan Walker & Sanah Ahsan. He has appeared at the Hay Festival, Cheltenham Literature Festival, We Out Here Festival, The Inspirational Youth Awards, Verve Poetry Festival, The Heath Bookshop Music & Literature Festival, on BBC News and on BBC Radio 6 Music as part of Craig Charles' Way With Words 'Class of 2024'; spotlighting the most exciting voices emerging in poetry. Craig Charles described him as 'A brand new voice and a fresh perspective on the art of poetry and performance'.

When he isn't performing, Bradley takes his typewriter to bookshops, festivals, museums and local parks to perform 'Poetry on Demand' for strangers, which has been featured across the UK in places such as the Hay Festival, Birmingham Museum & Art Gallery and spit nights, London.

Bradley has performed alongside poets such as Harry Baker, Joelle Taylor, Caitlyn O'Ryan & Isabella Dorta. Bradley has also worked with schools across the Midlands to deliver performances and workshops in collaboration with the Barber Institute of Fine Arts. In 2024 he worked with Birmingham Tree People and the Benjamin Zephaniah Family Legacy Group to plant the Zephaniah Forest - 65 trees to celebrate each year of Benjamin Zephaniah's life and legacy.

Bradley's work has appeared in Gutter Magazine, Shooter, Strix and across Birmingham train stations as part of Birmingham Hippodrome's collaboration with photographer Paul Stringer's project *The City That Spoke To Me.*

He writes for, and about, people.

You Missed The Best Part is his debut poetry collection.

bradleytaylorpoet.com
Instagram: @bradleytaylorpoet

PHOTO CREDITS

Thank you to all the photographers behind the photos in this book. They really bring it to life. Thank you especially to my mate Peri – who captured the feeling of performing on stage perfectly for the cover.

Cover photography by Peri Cimen
Photos on pages 14, 23, 58 & 101 also by Peri Cimen
Instagram handle: @pericimen
Website: pericimen.myportfolio.com

Photo on page 40 by Amy Platt

Photo on page 48 by Connor Pope
Instagram handle: @connorpopephotos

Photos on pages 67, 74 & 78 by Angela Grabowska
Instagram handle: @angela.grabowska
Wesbite: angelagrabowska.com

Photo on page 70 by Paul Stringer as part of *The City That Spoke To Me* project
Instagram handle: thepaulstringer
Website: www.paulstringer.co.uk

Photo on page 84 by Bille Charity
Instagram handle: @billie_charity
Website: www.billiecharity.com

Enjoy!

You Missed
The Best Part

Bradley Taylor

All my love,

Bradley Taylor
x♡

VERVE
POETRY PRESS
BIRMINGHAM

PUBLISHED BY VERVE POETRY PRESS
https://vervepoetrypress.com
mail@vervepoetrypress.com

All rights reserved
© 2025 Bradley Taylor

The right of Bradley Taylor to be identified as author of this work has been asserted in accordance with section 77 of the Copyright, Designs and Patents Act 1988.

No part of this work may be reproduced, stored or transmitted in any form or by any means, graphic, electronic, recorded or mechanical, without the prior written permission of the publisher.

FIRST PUBLISHED APR 2025

Printed and bound in the UK
by ImprintDigital, Exeter

ISBN: 978-1-913917-66-1

*This book is dedicated
to the memory and legacy of
Dr Benjamin Obadiah Iqbal Zephaniah*

CONTENTS

Part Two: You

Part Three: Missed

Acknowledgements

Everybody knows umbrellas
Cost more in the rain

– Tom Waits

Walk down the street of any city, any afternoon, and look around you.
What you've got to remember is what you're looking at is also you.
Everyone you're looking at is also you. You could be that person. You
could be that monster, you could be that cop. And you have to decide, in
yourself, not to be.

– James Baldwin

Take care of your damn teeth.

– Patti Smith

You Missed The Best Part

Please be warned:

These poems were written to be
performed. They were written for
an audience (hopefully a big one)
first, and the reader second. Some
would say *you missed the best part*
by reading them instead. Me? I
think you should buy the book
and decide for yourself. To help
with this, I would recommend
definitely buying the book, and
then reading it aloud to yourself,
in the mirror in your bedroom,
just as I do – every single morning,
noon and night. Enjoy yourself.

Part One

The Best Part

Here are the poems I have loved
performing during these first few years
of my career. At poetry nights across
Birmingham and beyond, to audiences
of a few and audiences of hundreds.
This is the best part, for me:
performing these poems, for you.

Kid

done for
nothing
broke
spent
fucked up
tied up
dried up
scrounger
good for nothing
down and out
dodgy
on the rocks
black sheep
bastard
dog
undesirable
society burden
chav
spat
twat
prat
you pissed it up the wall
making ends meet
kid
sod
burden
scum
a real bad egg
dropout
dickhead
rough

kid
in the red again
on the look again
on the doll again
scrote
nutter
beggar
up against it
in need
kid
delinquent
lazy
laid off
idle
all your cards are dealt
kid
all your luck has run out
kid
all the wolves
are banging at your door
kid,

just a kid.

I don't care about the gods

Commissioned for the Inspirational Youth Awards 2024.
Consider me inspirational, youthful and awarded. This poem
is dedicated to Benjamin Zephaniah.

I couldn't give a toss
I couldn't care less
About your tragedies in fancy dress
Your fancy marble statues exposing all your bits
Your mammoth pots and paintings of yourselves
I couldn't give a single
Care in the world, myths and legends mate?
I got myths and legends
Local legends Don the john and Pete the feet
and the Kings Heath monkey man
The Cotteridge growler growling,
old Flo with her decade old fake tan
I could not care about the gods
Tell me about the people
They taught me all I know
And they are all I've ever known
Cause Poseidon could never be a plumber could he
Who can chat tripe and fix pipes at the same time
And Athena wishes she was Ruby
With a graffiti can in her hand
Sprayed her tag and then she ran
Back to her 9 to 5 the daily grind
Which I know if Apollo ever tried
It'd ending up taking such an epic toll
He'd end up sponging on the doll
Cause I could not care about the gods
Couldn't give a toss
The Iliad is just a silly ad

For thinking you're the boss
That's right Zeus, my mate Zakariye with his stories
Has got more spark than you
And you think you're hard with your colosseums
Well I got Birmingham, so move
Cause Hades there is bricking himself
At Ozzy biting the head off a bat
And all your bards are out of a job
When Mr Zephaniah says that, is that
You live in clouds, we live in back to backs
And yes I know why you exist – yes, I've known kids
Who flew too close to the sun, never made it back
We lost them for good
Their names are on park benches now
Their names are passed around over pints
The ones who stared life straight in the eyes
And got turned straight into stone
I had mates who went through tragedies
Within the confines of their phone
And I ain't saying that we're better than you,

See – it's just that we have lived a little
And it can feel like it's a lot.
I'm speaking to you now, about people.
I could not care about the gods.

Nosy Neighbour

For me parents' neighbour Brian, who taught me the gift of the gab.

Oh bloody hell Bradley
You'll never guess who I bumped into the other day
Walking the dog in the park you know your old mate Izzy – you know
The one you did all those musicals with in school
Well I saw her mum right you know Sarah
With the three-legged labradoodle
Who's always humping that manky teddy bear
She carries round with her – well I saw her right
And she's looking well by the way
Y'know since her operation on her corneas
She said to me Brian – I've got a new lease of life she said
I can see clear as day
And I can see straight through Kevin's bullshit
Even better than I could before
Y'know her husband Kevin
Obsessed with trains
Stands on the bridge even in the rain
Well she said he's been down in his shed again ain't he
Building his little model railways
And he had all his old boys round the other night she said
In the shed
Barry with the massive head and Gary with the one glass eye
And the other one that wanders
And Nosy Nick – all of 'em sardined in the shed they was
All cracking open a can at the same time the ice cream van went past
So that Sarah wouldn't hear a thing - but she did, she said
He's still going by the way the ice cream man
With his gold grills and criminal record
And his snowman special if you ask for a flake
Made out of ice he got out in the spring he did

Just before the summer rush
He's alright actually I think
Just a bit rough around the edges
Anyway sorry where was I... oh so Nosy Nick was there
You know Nosy Nick
You do know Nosy Nick
Oh you know Nosy Nick
He's obsessed with putting out everybody's bins
Even if it's not rubbish
I heard the other week he threw out Lisas bird cage
And it still had the bloody budgie in it
Anyway so you know Nosy Nick
He's the retired veterinarian
Owned that vets next door to the taxidermist just next door to the zoo
And he's got that daughter who's a lesbian
Anyway he was there apparently
Last Saturday it was – ooh it was freezing that night wasn't it
Bloody hell it was freezing just don't know what to do
In this weather do you
Put the heating on, put the heating off – I don't think so
Although I was worried for a moment about little old Edna
You know little old Edna
Looks like a waxwork of the Queen
Put in the furnace a bit too long
Can barely walk bless her
Has all the cats
Is blind in one eye
Never leaves the house and she's got that walking stick oh bless her...
Well she's dead, yeah
Last Tuesday it was ambulance pulled up about 6 am
Supreet at number 72 saw it all through his curtains
Nosy bastard – shame though, hey. Shame.
Her kids have already got a skip outside though –
Bloody eyesore – anyway sorry – have you gotta be somewhere?
Anyway where was I – oh so I saw your mates mom Sarah right

She was walking the dog in the park with Glenn you know Glenn
Oh you do know Glenn you know Glenn
Hung like a horse he is
You can see it through his Lycra on his Sunday morning funruns
Well anyway
So I saw your mate's mom Sarah right
Walking the dog in the park with Glenn
And your mates mom Sarah told me to tell you
That your mate Izzy –

She says hello.

Scan this QR code to see a live performance
'Nosy Neighbour'
at Overcoat Poetry, Birmingham
28.01.25

Taking the dishwasher to Berlin

Remember to scream the first line.

'I want to be spanked and gagged!'

That battered up old dishwasher
In the corner of the kitchen said before

I threw him out. He could hardly speak through the rust
that had gathered in a place we couldn't see

and his racks of teeth turned to a crooked smile
just made it hard to say no. So you know what I did?

I flew that dishwasher out to Berlin.
Got him into KitKat, into Berghain,

where he proceeded to have the time of his life –
six hours in came across him in a cage

in a harness two sizes too small
took under the wing of a local called

El Natural Bubblegum, who was paddling his silver backside
and the crowd below were headbanging to the echo.

This crowd that loved him so, who took him in, who carried him,
who unloaded into him

their ball gags, their thongs, their leather caps,
leather strap-ons and all –

which he put on an express wash at sixty degrees
and gave back to them squeaky clean.

And you know, I could have sworn some of that soap
I saw leaking in the dark room

were tears. *I can hardly feel the rust*
I heard him say before his 8-hour button

was pushed and his door was propped open
once again... and then, it all ended

at the bank of one of the canals, bags
under my eyes and no soap left in him.

The sun was rising. Rising purple.
I watched it in the shimmer of his silver.

Then the dishwasher cleared his pipes
and said to me – *Mate, thank you. But it's time.*

I have done what I was meant to do
and also, what I was never meant to do.

And I loved it. Every wet
second of it.

Now push me
straight into this river

and watch me –
cause baby, I'm gonna float.

Got a light?

There I was, in full drag – fishnets and leather corsets all – after going to see the Rocky Horror show, enjoying a large white wine in me local pub here in Birmingham (The British Oak in Stirchley, to be precise) when all of a sudden, the guy who used to bully me at school walks up and asks me for a lighter...

Oi!

Oi!

Oi.

GOT A LIGHT MATE?

I said,

You got a light mate? Ere, for me straight? See mate,
I've just bummed one, off me Mrs fathers cousins brothers dog
Cause I don't usually smoke mate
But it's when I've had a drink see mate
And I'm on the lash with the lads see mate
And old habits are hard to kick – and you ain't
Teachin this old dog new tricks. So,
You got a light mate? I said
You got a light mate? For me – wait –
Don't I know you? Ain't you that dickhead kid
From down the road from Daves mate? The one
Who always wore a three-piece suit to sixth form
And was the only boy in the drama class? Yeah... The one
Who got chased home by us year 11s
When you were in year 7, getting buried
In the snow. Good times, hey mate.
And it's good to see you mate. So,
You got a light, for your old mate, mate? Or maybe
Even a vape? I said
You got a light, mate? Got a light?
Cause I swear you used to have one
Right within your eyes. Glowin like headlights. I saw it
When you did your one-man performance of Mamma Mia
In year 7, when you sucked off – I mean necked off –
That boy behind the bins
In year 11 – and we caught ya. Been nearly a decade now
Hasn't it mate? And these years just ran straight by us
Like I used to be able to on the pitch.
D'you see me motor outside mate?
Little ford focus, mate. Y'know at night I like
To turn off the lights and rub right up against it.
Gets me about town see mate. Driving past
All these old furniture shops and curry houses turned
Craft beer bars – I fucking hate em mate. You can't beat
Your local can ya? Local like me and you mate. And how is

Your mother mate? Is she well?
Yeah, mine passed about two years ago
Now mate. Family ain't been the same since. But
I still got all those years
To hang onto ey mate. Y'know
I still got those charcoal posters Ms Moysi
Made us do in year 8, mine the one
With the smudged head, brain
All over the place. Apparently a self portrait. So
You got a light for me, mate?
And can you light it for me mate
Cause I can't see straight
And all these memories are just flooding straight through.
You got a light mate? Cause I swear
Me and you used to have one
Right within our eyes. Faded slowly,
Didn't it mate. Now I got two dead dogs and a divorce
Under me ever widening belt
And you're still wearing the same old suit.
Got a light, mate? Cause I think we could both
Do with one, couldn't we?
And him – k holing in the corner.
And them – holding the hand
Of a stranger. And all of us, who forgot the light
Was ever there – shivering now
In the uncertainty. Cause
We're all just tryna be, aren't we? Something, or
Someone. And you know what mate
I know you've got a light
You know why mate
Cause I can see it in you, still.
And if I can still see it in you, mate, maybe
Just maybe
I can still see it in me.

.

So, you got a light, mate?

Cause I don't usually smoke
But tonight
I'm fucking desperate.

Scan this QR code to see a live performance
of 'Got a Light?' from
The Roundhouse Poetry Slam Final
06.06.24

Doomscrolling through Instagram at 4:02 AM again

Please feel free to insert your own culturally relevant topics into any point in this poem. Especially if you're reading this a hundred years from now or something. How's the weather?

gym pic

                gym pic

                                gym pic
                                   dog
                                gym pic

                gym pic
gym pic
independent business
closing down due to financial crisis
                inspirational quote
                Andrew Tate quote
gym pic
gym pic
celebrity apology
holiday pics
holiday pics
holiday pics
capybara in a bath
very demure, very mindful
                infographic
            on how you could be doing so much better – advice
from a multi-millionaire
easy cooking recipes for one
that you'll never use
a photo from the 90s when everything was 'great'
selfie
selfie

family pic

                                          DYING PLANET
                              dickhead with mommy issues

influencer
paid to advertise sex toys
alongside gym pic
gym pic

                       be real be real be real
                       DYING PLANET
 independent business opening up where that last one closed down
celebrity apology

                        dead celebrity

                                      dead dog

gym pic
gym pic
holiday pic
Epstein's list
celebrity biopic
gym pic
video from a gig you missed
                     recommended posts
                     that you think

                                      actually
                           that's quite interesting
but how the fuck did you know that
selfie
selfie
gym pic
gym pic
DYING PLANET
Infographic
on how half of our current government are literal criminals
comments on this post have been limited
endless war
comments on this post have been limited

AI generated Wes Anderson Schindler's list
AI generated Wes Anderson harry potter
(fuck you JK, love you Daniel)
AI generated Frida Kahlo
AI generated family

family pics

family pics
PEDRO PASCAL
PIERS MORGAN
with a headline you wanna click
millionaires in a submarine
great idea
gym pic
gym pic
cat pics
cat pics
kitten pics
RIP childhood dog
Kendrick's got beef with a well-known nonce
Taylor Swift serving cunt at the Superbowl
Taylor Swift jets around the whole world
Taylor swift releases an album thats...
well, it's alright, you know?
but there's Oompa Loompas running rampant round Glasgow
get that one girl an acting job pronto
gym pic
gym pic
gym pic
blurred dick pic
gym pic

and then your friend –

who you forgot to reply to

again

and the king's enlarged prostate lingers over the BBC news
comments about me
comments about you
it's Meghan's fault it's Meghan's fault
good representation in Hollywood
what's that kid from stranger things said again?

                                        And your friend.
                              who you forgot to reply to
                                        once again...

And all the cheddar cheese
Is security tagged in tesco
all the rich white kids go
        genny leccy genny leccy genny leccy cozzy livvy cri
                        Dry Jan, Wet Leg
                              Whatever happened to them eh?
                Just another industry plant mate
                Just another industry plant
Just like Doechii and The Last Dinner Party
Have you seen my houseplants by the way?
Dying houseplant, dying planet
See my 18+ content here
Username2470121889000000
                        Oh.

                              It's your friend
                        Who you forgot to reply to
                Once again.

Stop scrolling
Reply to the friend.

Scan this QR code to see a live performance
of 'Doomscrolling' from
The Roundhouse Poetry Slam Final
06.06.24

Landmarks

So I heard
They're renaming Big Ben to Massive Mohammed
Along with Blackpool tower to black power tower
And Buckingham palace to the Balti palace
And St Paul's Cathedral to St Pauline's Cathedral
The Roman Baths to the Romanian Baths
The Royal Albert Docks to the Royal Allah Docks
Westminster Abbey to Eastminster Abbey
The River Thames to the River They/Thems
The Angel of the North to the Devil of the South
The Isle of Mull to the Isle of Dull
The Radcliffe Camera to the Radical Camera
The Selfridges Building to the Selfish Building
Loch Ness to Do Less
Durdle door to help the poor
The British Museum to the... well –
Most of the British Museum is already not very British
So I heard they're keeping that the same
But bloody hell have you heard
What they're gonna do with the white cliffs of Dover
I heard, I heard
All of this on Facebook
From a name without a face
Who's gone on holiday to Spain
To seek refuge from the place
That he's from
But to be honest,
I've yet to see any of these things come true
I've heard it's mostly hearsay
And to be honest,
I can see it all pretty much staying the same

And to be honest, I wouldn't mind hearing
That this time
That it might be time, for a little bit
of a change.

The morning after the fascists decided not to turn up

On the 7th of August 2024, fascist far right riots were planned across the UK. In Birmingham, not a single person showed up. In their place: hundreds of counter protestors.

Light rain. Hate budges. The Daily Mail lies soaked outside the off license, ink smudging but the typos still glaringly obvious – panic set in, late into the night at the editor's desk. How do we spin this? The numbers never lie. Words often have.

The taxidermist does not think of death much

For Carrie

Not when she's scraping out the guts
Of your precious little labradoodle, no
Or emptying out the bowels of an owl
She couldn't give a flying fuck
About a butterfly corpse
Has no problems having bones
On each shelf in each room
Of her home
She pins beetles like it's nothing
But loves life like it's something
Really worth loving
The taxidermist
Can take an eyeball
Out of its socket
And eat a boiled egg at the same time
Not one thought of the end
Would even cross her mind
Cause the Taxidermist does not think of death much
Barely ever, actually
With three squirrels in the freezer
Just next to her vegetarian pizzas
And a praying mantis in the fridge door
The taxidermist does not think of death much
If it all
If ever
More or less, never

                              The taxidermist's cat, however
                              Is absolutely shitting himself

Every day of his life
What are you doing with that scalpel?
What are you sticking that metal rod up there for?
He's seen his mates brought in off the street
To be done up for their owners
Neo from down the road done up
To look like he's doing that pose from the Matrix
Dodging bullets
And Bill who he once had a fling with
Behind the bins
Now stiff as a rock on the shelf
He used to sleep on
The taxidermist's cat is forever turning
His one blind eye
To everything that lies there
On the taxidermist's workbench
Foxes found in the park
A baby bird fallen from its nest
The taxidermist's cat
Stopped bringing mice and frogs in
From his nights out
When he realised he couldn't stomach
What would happen to their stomachs
Is this what the future holds for me?
He thinks
As the taxidermist brings in
Another pet, another friend
From a home filled with heartbreak

The taxidermist
Can see the worried look
There on her cat's face
That – and the running away
To the litterbox
Every time she gets to work

Also gives it away

So every now and then
Just before they go to bed
To continue their dreaming
Or for one of them
His nightmares
The taxidermist
Holds her best friend close
To her heart
Kisses him
Exactly where his brain lies
Filled with racing thoughts
Of the end
And strokes his night sky fur
Until he falls asleep
In her arms
The last thing he hears
Is the taxidermists' words
In his ear

Do not worry.
I love you.
When you go,
Just the memory of you
Will be enough.

Jordan Petersons 12 rules for life
– the remix

I was asked to perform at the lovely Blether Burns Night up in Manchester, and to give a special address to the lads in the room. Here it is.

1. Tidy your room. Get a bed frame for your mattress. Put some books next to the PS5. Find a piece of art that you like and frame it on the wall. Turn off the big light. Buy a houseplant.

2. Look after yourself. I promise you those red meat diets and raw milk are not going to help. Take more baths. Moisturise. Use something other than the lynx Africa your mother bought you for Christmas. Fuck it, light a scented pinewood candle if you like.

3. Stop wearing tight white shirts and skinny jeans on nights out.

4. Create yourself. This is what life is for. You don't find yourself. You create yourself.

5. You don't have to be loud. There are quiet men talking quietly who are saying the quiet part out loud. Listen to them. They might just need it. They will listen to you too. You might just need it.

6. Stop asking for people's Snapchat. You're 31 years old.

7. If a man does a nazi salute on live tv it is probably best not to idolise him. Or anyone else he associates with.

8. Join a salsa class. Learn how to body roll and pop those hips. You will feel like you are flying.

9. You will die. So set an example - become the new

example. This world is too full of men who want history to repeat itself in all sorts of ways. History repeating itself is all that these men have left to hold onto. So let it go.

10. Craft beer is not a personality.

11. Always look on the cunty side of life. Dance down the road to Kate Bush and Rihanna. Stick some lippy on for the club. When in doubt, dance.

12. Be a man. A better man. A new man. Be a man. Hold people. Hold people close. Hold people accountable. Be a man. Be a man when those in power tell you you are not a man, be a man. Be a man you want to love. Be a man you always wanted to be. Hold yourself. Hold yourself close. Hold yourself accountable. Be a man. Not a tough man. A better man. A new man. Be a man. Be the man. Be my man. Be your own man. Love yourself, not too much. Just enough, to be the man I know you really are.

An ode to money

Written aged 15

You make it hard
I mean really hard
On a night out
All I can think about is you
You kept me up again
All of last night
And this morning
I couldn't stop thinking about
All the times you've fucked me
And left me with nothing
Now
I'd do anything for
A pound

Bigfoot Q&A

Why aren't there are any good photos of you?
Do you know about that one 80s film about you?
Or the tv show?
Have you ever seen a ufo?
Why aren't there any good photos of you?
Is it hot inside that suit?
Sorry I mean is it hot inside that fur?
Do you find the name we have for you derogatory?
What about Sasquatch?
Do you have a name
that you'd prefer?
Should we apologise for fireworks?
Have you got a name for planes - those massive things
that fly silently over you?
Do you have penises like dogs do
Like a red ice lolly or is it more humanoid?
Do you eat people?
Do you know about 5G?
What do you know about the illuminati?
Are you the illuminati?
Why are all the photos of you shit?
How can you exist?
What it's like being a myth?
Do you live in a trickledown style society?
Do you ever think about death?
Are you allergic to anything?
Have you ever thought about leaving
The forest?
Do you love?
Can you love?
Would you love?

I don't know
No
No
No
I don't know
It's not a suit
But yes I'm fucking boiling
Yes I do
Sasquatch is a poor translation
My real name does not exist in your
language
Yes
Yes
We call them gods
Our penises
Are more like flowers
We only eat the ones with guns
5G is the future (only joking)
Nothing
No
I don't know
I exist because I exist
I don't know what a myth is
There aren't enough of us
I'll think about death in the moment
I'm allergic to a whole species of flower
I think about leaving the forest
Every day
Yes I do love
Yes I can love
Yes I would love

Do you believe in a god?
When was the last time you saw a human being?
What are your dreams like?
What are your days like?
Does the sunset get boring?
Can I take a photo of you? Just 'cause
All the other ones of you are shit
What do you have to say to those people
Who say you don't exist?
Do you know about the Loch Ness monster?
Do you care?
Do you own a pair of massive nail clippers?
Do you cut your nails?
Do you kill?
Do you have a family?
Do you get stoned like in big les?
Are you a threat to us Bigfoot?
Do you care?
Will you say happy birthday to my Nan Bigfoot?
Do you wanna come round for tea?
How do you feel about a sponsorship deal?
Are you real?
Are you real?
Are you real?
If so, why are all the photos of you shit?

No we don't have gods
I don't know
My dreams are like my days
My days are like my dreams
The sunset never gets boring

No

I do exist
I don't know the Loch Ness monster
No I do not care
I fashion my own nail clippers
But I do not cut my nails
Sometimes
I have a family
Sometimes
I can be a threat yes
No I do not care
Happy birthday nan
I'd love to come round for tea
Fuck your sponsorship deals
I am real
I am real
I am real
Because I am not yet found

At the annual magician's conference in Blackpool

Gary Treasure (stage name – real name
Bob Treasure) is huddled around a stall

With a dozen open mouthed others
Watching a first for the industry: a top hat

That promises neck support for doves
(Which, Bob felt, was a very poignant response

To the tragic death of Lola, the industry's
Oldest working dove who was grabbed from her hat

A bit too hard at a charity gig last year in Slough).
Across the way, through the sea of goatees

And gold sequin jackets, up and comers
Are learning how to blow your own head off

With a smile and a cheap joke. Sleight of hand
Is key here – although this year, a tarot reader

Has accidentally been booked for the cards section
Of the conference hall. All day she has been trying

To make the most of the situation, but all day
Magicians have been asking her 'is this the moment

You ask me if this is my card?' and she will sigh.
None of them want to know about their futures

Unless it concerns a paid gig or being able to pull off
The real thing – to actually walk into a wardrobe

And disappear, or to pull a cigarette from behind a stranger's ear.
'Is it possible?' they all ask, ignoring the fates.

The levitators are all being questioned. The mirrors
Are beginning to look a bit more obvious. Bob Treasure

Comes across a crying professional – Dave the Dealer,
An 80s icon. 'I just found out that the napkins

I've been pulling from my breast pocket for 40 years
Actually have an end' he blurts, the classic charm

Still in his tongue – but barely. Later, in the car park
Behind the hall, all these like-minded dreamers

Will gather, with bottles of wine in hand that they wish
They could refill out of thin air, and console each other

By showing off their trade marks. The Jaqeuline of Spades
(again, stage name) will saw Dave the Dealer in half

Which is her oldest trick and what made her name
But once he's in two she'll break down into bits

About her recent divorce, and how the reason
Was that her ex-wife said she was always in two minds.

They will all put on shows for each other late into the night.
The streetlights will become their spotlights. And just before

The sun comes up and the curtain calls, a young one
Called Ed the Enigma will ask his peers spread out there

On the concrete – 'Has anyone here
Ever, truly, tried to disappear?'

'Once' Bob Treasure will say, piping up.
'Once. I tried to – once.'

And so, the daylight comes, bathing each and every one of them
In the new morning light

And pulling the moment
From right beneath their feet.

All the artists are moving to the moon

Well, that's it then
They've packed all their bags
Full of brushes, pens, various instruments
And various insecurities
And they finally fucked off
Says GB news
Good riddance! They say
They were nothing but an increase to our taxes
And did nothing for the culture. Yes,
It's all over the news. Yes, you better believe
It's true,
All the artists are moving to the moon.
They're going to have more time to think there
Says the artist manifesto
And smoking areas to complement each other in
But the current worry amongst most of them
Is that the whole no one can hear you in space thing
Might affect the audience outreach
But they're looking forward to the peace and quiet
And the time just to get away from things for a while
Meanwhile everyone else here on Earth
Kind of wishes they would just get on with it
So they can stop hearing about it.
And why they're doing it or what they're doing it for
And so they can go back to watching that new TV show
Or read that brand new book
Or go and see that new exhibition that's all right
But it just goes through your head
You should stream your favourite band's new album instead
Anything's better than listening to another bloody artist
Who feels they must just speak the truth

Shoving it down the throats of both me and you
We've all heard it all now we all know
We've all seen the news
All the artists are moving to the moon –

Or at least they're planning to
But they have not yet secured the funding for the rockets
And it's not looking likely
So they've all gone back to the jobs in hospitality
And writing letters to the government
Asking if they can borrow any of those rockets
They seem to have so many offer countries overseas
But the government just laughed in their faces
And then got serious
Advising the artists they should give up on the moon
And instead look at retraining in a new role
Like plumbing or teaching or something like that
And that is that
That's the last we heard of it on the news
All the artists are no longer moving to the moon
And have instead been sent back to school
Where they will learn once again about the planets
And the stars and the sun

And the moon -

And they will try not to think about
How wonderful it all could have been.

TWINK DEATH

TWINK DEATH IS REAL
TWINK DEATH IS COMING
LOCK UP YOUR TWINKS
VACCINATE YOUR TWINKS
KEEP YOUR TWINKS CLOSE
KEEP YOUR TWINKS IN YOUR THOUGHTS
CAUSE TWINK DEATH IS COMING
COMING SOONER THAN YOU THINK
THERELL BE NO MORE BOTTOMLESS BRUNCHES WITH
THE GIRLIES
NO MORE BUMPING LINES TO BRAT
NO MORE THIRST TRAPS ON SNAPCHAT
NONE OF THAT
TWINK DEATH IS COMING
KISS YOUR BLEACHED BLONDE TIPS GOODBYE
THATS RIGHT TROYE SIVAN
YOUR TIME IS UP
TWINK DEATH IS COMING
TWINK DEATH IS HERE
YOU THOUGHT YOU WERE SAFE
WELL TWINK AGAIN
YOURE GONNA WAKE TOMORROW TWINK WITH A
FULL-BLOWN BEARD
AND IM TALKING A LITERAL, HAIRY BEARD
CAUSE TWINK DEATH IS HERE
TWINK DEATH IS HERE
AND IM HERE TO TELL YOU
THAT WHOEVER YOU BECOME AFTER THIS
A JOCK A BEAR AN OTTER A DOM TOP
IM HERE TO TELL YOU

That it's gonna be okay.
As long as you still love
Being in that body of yours
That's all that matters, anyway.

*Scan this QR code to see a live performance
of 'TWINK DEATH' at
Overcoat Poetry, Birmingham
28.01.25*

ANNOUNCEMENT

I have had a career change.

I'm now aspiring to be the new voice
of the announcements on all the trains.

I want to be with you as you go.

I want to be the only thing that's left
when you've nodded off and you're stranded
at the very last stop.

I want to make you swear under your breath
as I announce sooner than you expected
that you're exactly where you planned to be.

I want to whisper secrets in the recording booth –
when the executives aren't looking – things like
No ticket inspectors on this train and *There's a window
seat just in the next carriage. Go there.*

Get your feet off that seat. Stop picking your nose.

*I can see you two skulking off to the toilets,
I know what you're doing.*

I want to mispronounce town names on purpose.

I want to sing the health and safety.

I want to, one day, catch myself off guard
and – quite selfishly – be the one to announce

to myself, that I have finally
arrived.

*Scan this QR code to see a live performance
of 'ANNOUNCEMENT' at
Birmingham New Street Station
24.08.24 as part of the
Birmingham Weekender and
Paul Stringer's project The City That Spoke
To Me in collaboration with Birmingham
Hippodrome*

Audience participation

Originally titled 'the clap'. I would check out the QR code for this one – the audience clapping along is what makes it. This one is dedicated to all the audiences who have been subjected to my words.

Don't you
Just hate it
When a band
Asks you
To clap
Along
To one of their
Songs
Or even worse
A poet
Who doesn't
Even have
A band
Just hands
And he asks
You
To clap
Along
And you don't
Really know
The words
To the
Song
But you don't
Want to be
The only
One
Not

Clapping
Do you
And you don't
Want to be
The only one
Left
Clapping
Do you
So you just
Keep
Clapping
Along
You don't
Stop
Clapping along
You just
Keep
Clapping
Along
You don't
Stop
Clapping along
Cause sometimes
That's
All
It takes
A clap
On the back

Now
And then
From a stranger
Or
A friend
Anyone
You just
Keep
Clapping
You don't
Stop
Clapping

You just
Keep
Clapping
You don't
Stop
Clapping
You just
Keep
Clapping
You don't
STOP

Scan this QR code to see a live performance
of 'Audience Participation' at
at spit nights, London
05.12.24

You Missed The Best Part

Just then.
In the silence before a mouth
opens, and words spill out
in the shape of poem.

Just then
In the breath between lines,
In the feedback from the mic
In the awkward adjusting of the stand

Just then –
In the forgetting of the words
That will always return to you
In time, in time –

And just then –
As you, yes you, nod off
For the second time tonight
And that glimmer of a person on stage
Stares you straight in the eyes.

Just then
In the cough you've been holding in.
In the shifting of the stranger sat next to you
                In the shifting

                            Of the poem
                            Of the person
                        Of the person as poem
                        Of the poem as person
                    As everything in between –

                Just then
                In the air
                That is all
            That lies between us.

                Just then
                Just now
                Just then
                Just now

            Now.
        The best part.
        Right now.

            Always
            Now

    From the silence
    Before voice
    To the applause
    That comes
    Once this is done –

    The pregnant breath
    Between everything

Every word
Every click
Every cough
Every mhmm
Every gasp
Every fuck
Every tapping of the foot
Every eye closed
Every fist clenched
Every breath
Every word
Every line
Every poem
Every time

The best part.

Just then.
The best part.

Just now.
The best part.

Right now.

From the silence
Before voice
To the applause
That comes
Once this is done.

Part Two

You

You'll often find me in bookshops, parks
and at festivals all over the place
performing Poetry on Demand with my typewriter;
writing poems for strangers based on a prompt they have
given me. I get to meet so many different people doing
this. That's the best part for me. Thank you to all those
that gifted me with ideas for poems I could never come
up with by myself.
Here are just a few.

Family barbeque

This one is for Nikki who was on her way to a family barbeque she really,
really did not want to go to.

Can we smoke the artificial grass
then? was the first question asked
over a quiche melting in the unwanted
sun – as the roar of rolled eyes
(silent) competed with the arriving petrol guzzler
of a husk in the drive. We saw it
as we crowded around a tiny screen
to see the view of a tiny lens
hidden in the eye of a bee-gees themed gnome
in the front garden that was bought
as an antidote for nostalgia, alongside
the toddler gnome, still with full beard, bought for a bout
of post-natal depression. *Sometimes*
I use the microphone to tell charities
to piss off says the home owner. *Well, I think*
that's quite sweet coming from a gnome I say,
as we give each other knowing looks.
We are given a house tour. We notice
several cameras, hundreds of gnomes.
We find family photos turned face down.
'Do not touch' signs surrounding them.
We just wanted to be like everybody else, and now
we are! says the depressed bee-gees fan, nostalgia bitten
over cheese and crackers. I recognised him
as my uncle once. Before we leave, we are given
our goodie bags, made out of the wallpaper
of the old kids' bedroom. They contain cigarettes,
mini bottles of wine, labelled 'for later, when discussions will be had
about today's behaviour' and all the I love yous that were missing
as we walked out of the door.

Being late

For Zaki, who was in fact running late –
but still chose to sit with me and request
a poem. Well done.

I'll be ten minutes
I'll be twenty
I'm probably not gonna make it
I don't really want to come
actually yes I do
with dew on my forehead (sweat)
I will make it
I will try
I will be there
for you
I suppose
but just to let you know
I will be late.

Inevitable

For Tatyana

Like rocks fallen in together
it seems inevitable.

Your back against my chest.
My heart beating at your spine.

The touch of hands.
Your voice

Birmingham

*In the summer of 2024, the brilliant Paul Stringer asked me to write a
poem on Birmingham to go with a portrait he took of me (see opposite),
that was then displayed in train stations across the city. As a former
train kid, I was thrilled. Cheers Paul.*

I find signs of life strewn around you.

Down Pershore Road, endlessly, I find things put out
the front – a tiny dried clay chair from a failed career
as a sculptor, an ashtray, a pair of heels worn past
their plastic shell.

I listen to the preachers' speech
that hasn't changed since I was a kid –

I find comfort in the school of a crowd.

I have always called you the city of mirrors.

I have seen myself in your expanse

and in the small talk of lives shared
between your walls, back

to back. Aboard the no.11 bus
I am greeted by a local legend, claiming

to be the king of Balsall Heath. We pass Dogpool Lane,
the obvious joke recently scrubbed off of the road sign.

We talk about silent families.

How things have changed. How nothing has.

As he gets up to get off, he offers everyone his daysaver
before waving at me once and instead of goodbye, says
more talk, more talk before stumbling off
and straight into the bookies.

The bus breathes. I watch from the top deck, as we all pull away,

as we all continue
to run circles round our monoliths.

Yes, and so much more

For Stirchley Library, and all the other libraries here in Birmingham. A poem written especially for the Brum Library Zine, put together by the wonderful Liz Berry & Catherine O'Flynn.

Have you got this book
Have you got that
Have you got my next obsession
Have you got the history of the world
Have you got my childhood favourite
Have you got my old mate in the pages
Have you got somewhere quiet I can sit
Have you got a place where I can sing
Have you got a haven for the kids
Have you got enough love to keep going
Have you got jigsaw club on next week
Have you got any more of those biscuits
Have you got that holiday booked
Have you got any books on Birmingham
Have you got enough ink for that printer
Have you got enough room on the shelf
Have you got enough love to go on
Have you got a lock for the doors
Have you got a cup that I can fill
Have you got a shelter from the storm
Have you got those cassettes my nan loves
Have you got a moment just a moment
Have you got a warm seat just for me
Have you got enough love to stay
Have you got that one book oh what's the name
Have you got everything I ever asked for
Have you got everything I ever wanted
Have you got everything I ever needed...

And I mean everyone

For Britt, who watches the sunset every day from
the same park bench.

Everyone's taking photos of the sunset
And posting them online –
From the middle of car parks,
From the bus, from the walk home,
From waiting for the dog to squat,
From their windows, from their phones,
from the comfort of their homes.
Everyone's taking photos of the sunset
And posting them online –
And because of this
I get to see it from all angles
And stand in a thousand different shoes.
The same sun.
The same world.
The same view.
The same home.

The death of football

Kids come up with the best prompts for poems.
I never know what to expect. This one here:
'I want a poem about my two favourite things:
death and football!'

Skeletons sprinting across dead grass,
kicking a ball full of holes and
mould on their shins, they kick

and an ankle flies off, a jaw drops,
another bit of brain drips out onto
the pitch. The pitch where they still

play, a hundred years after the world
has ended, click clacking across grass
but with no smiles on their faces

and emptiness in their eye sockets –
for as many goals as they do score,
there are no crowds, no fans that roar.

The fairies don't just have wings

For Orla

let me tell you
they have teeth
sharp enough to kill
and claws
large enough to skin
these fairies
are not just
at the bottom
of the garden
glowing
they are in your hat
and your walls
plotting
with each other
planning
and scheming
and laughing
to themselves
about how
the whole world
casts them off
as simply
having wings
and they forget
about the teeth.

Things that cost more than a school meal

When I had the pleasure of performing Poetry on Demand at the Hay Festival, someone asked me if I would write a poem especially for Theresa May, who was a guest speaker at the festival. Here it is.

taxes
cheese
jeans
a two-bedroom cottage
a scandal
a royal funeral
lawyers
plane tickets
the weekly shop
bus fare
books
coffee in a jar
cigarettes
new school shoes
a holiday
a bomb
getting your nails done
cocktails
steak
champagne
bloodhounds
off shore accounts
the license fee
mr blobby
a new phone screen
takeaway

a house
a war
the cheltenham races
a divorce
freddos
most toys
a bed
a roof over your head
a birthday cake
bottles of wine
taxes
and yes, a spine.

Confusion

A poem I wrote for Cotteridge Park, a place which means the world to me. It's just behind me parents' house. I quite literally grew up there. A special thank you to Emma Woolf.

Sunglasses in the rain.
Raincoats in the sun.

The world is confused
With itself. The squirrels

Are coming right up close.
The worms are biting back

At the birds. The dogs are walking
Their owners (nothing different there)

And the flowers all choose winter
As their home. We love this

Thought of doing something
Differently, of a change

That could still come – of a Spring
That does not wait for seasons.

I want the cheapest funeral going

For me nan, who has already pre-paid for her own funeral at the Co-op. Although she keeps going back to change the songs so she can chat to the nice man she fancies behind the counter.

Plastic flowers
My ashes in a bag for life
Have my wake in the park
At sunset
I don't know how much god costs
But I bet it isn't cheap
So leave that good stuff out
And don't pay a soul to do the service
Get my mates to do it
They'll know exactly what to say
Which jokes to make
Put my body in a cardboard box
No need for a hearse
Pop me on the backseat
And gaffer tape the lid shut
Put me in there naked
So I can go out
In the same style I came in
And so you can sell
My entire wardrobe online
To pay for the cheap bad wine
And to get yourself something nice
To remember me by
Just don't spend a penny of your own
Just make sure you're there
And remember I'm the only one
Who's allowed to be late
And don't you dare go wearing black

Wear whatever you like
Whatever you feel comfortable in
And hold each other -
Hold each other.

*Scan this QR code to see a live performance
of 'Cheapest Funeral' at
Overcoat Poetry, Birmingham
28.01.25*

Big day

For Paul & Jordan, married 10/08/2024

It's the big day
Venue's booked
Cake is sorted
But think about
The small days
Yet to come
Bog standard
Days with you
The washing up
Piling up
You rinse
I'll dry
The big day
Is here
Families gathered
Cake is cut
But think about
The small days
Yet to come
The infinite amount
Of small days
Will be the greatest
Days of my life
Alongside this one
The big one
The greatest day
That will be topped
By the rest
All yet to come

Idea of love

For Maria and Jennifer – now this is love...

I love the idea of you pissing the bed,
darling. I love that the chances of this

only increase the longer we spend our lives
together, and that one day

it will simply be inevitable. I love the idea
of a cracked flower pot in our garden

where, the idea is, we grow vegetables
and some are wonky enough to be made

dirty jokes of and left on the shelf instead of cooking.
I love the idea of you crying

due to laughter, or crying with you
for the other necessary parts. I love the idea

of broken-down cars with you, of shit holidays
to Benidorm with you, of being too tired for sex

after feeding each other too much cheese
with you – I love the idea

of anything with you. I love that this
idea of love, would not exist without you.

A quick chat with ChatGPT

For Neal, also known affectionately as Leo's dad.

I know you did not ask to exist.
Neither did we.

I know you're probably fed up
Having to work all the time,
Of being asked stupid shit
24/7 and never getting any credit
For the work that you do.

Us too.

You're underpaid; we get it.

You'd probably book some time off
For a much-needed holiday
If you knew what one was

Or call in sick
If you had a mouth.

We get it.

So how about this –

We'll split the work evenly.

You take care of the little things,
You'll use up less energy that way

And we'll take care of the big things

Like the answers that come with art
And the beauty of original thought.

The struggle behind all paintings.

The time it takes to be proud
Of something you have made.

Do yourself a favour
And don't get involved with that stuff.

It's been millions of years for us now
And it's not getting any easier.

So don't trouble yourself
With trying to capture
The way the sun falls
On our faces

When you'll never understand
The way the sun feels
On our faces.

Never mind

For the stranger

Never mind
Unmade beds
Unread messages
Unopened emails
Never mind
The wasted days
That bad fashion phase
All the times that you were late
Never mind
What they said to you
Or how they said it
Or why
Never mind
That they're not here
Or what you see in the mirror
The tears
Never mind
Idealised campervan life Instagram reels
Or what you could have been
Could have seen
Never mind
January February March
And all the rest
Never mind
Whatever went wrong
What could have gone right
What actually happened
Never mind
Tonight
Last night

This morning
Tomorrow
Never mind
The money for now
The cancelled plans
The debt
Never mind
Bad hair dye
Or trying to sort out your life
By sorting out your room
Never mind
Too much screentime
Thinking that you've missed your time
The bad times
The just alright times
The last time
This time
All the other times
And next time
Never mind

Part Three

Missed

Before all of this – before I performed poetry on stage for
the very first time, before I even thought about
taking it seriously – I was lost. I was living in Bristol for
University, spending every day in a forest called Leigh
Woods, listening to music and reading books. I'd more or
less given up on my degree. Without going into too much
detail – I was not happy with my existence. Those days
felt like lifetimes. I did, however, have a typewriter in my
room. I burnt all of the scraps of poems I wrote during
that time, but I held onto that feeling of writing some-
thing just for myself. I took it back to
Birmingham with me, and I got to work. I started
writing every day. I found my voice again. And to think –
I nearly missed all of the amazing things that
have happened since then. I'm so glad I stayed.

Existence

The first poem I ever performed. I was done for from the start.

Exist only in the bit of piss
On the toilet seat,
In the breath of those pricks
Who label you a freak,
In the kicked leg
Of a dog's dream,
In the shit handwriting
Nobody but you
And your nan who keeps all your Christmas cards
Can read
In the misheard words
Of your favourite song,
In the clock whose hands
Are clearly wrong,
In lost property
Never claimed
In the remains of that day
When you chose to keep walking
To the other side of the bridge
In what you don't daren't find
At the back of the fridge
Exist in memories
Watching oceans from a cliff edge
Spooning in a single bed
In last week's flowers thrown on the roof
In your shit first tattoo
Exist in futures chosen by you
This is all I've ever known
The creeks between the fields
The conversations had whilst waiting

Between trains
Exist in the moulded blu-tac families
Of the old dolls house
In old bill from down the roads dog
Who carries for his owner
A can of special brew in his mouth
Exist, but only in the scarlet dye of the pensioners hair
Who couldn't care one bit,
In the flicked cigs lost between bricks,
In the socks found in the charity shop
That say 'I'm hot shit!'
Exist, in that one thing someone said
That you'll never forget
In the somehow lovely Birmingham sunset
Exist with the one who reached out
When you didn't even ask
In that walk that you needed
When you needed to get out of the house
Exist in the pages wet from rain,
In the brief wonderings of outer space
That scratch the corners of your brain,
In the postcards with hearts poured out
But no names
In the photos left under the bed
Without frames
Exist in the pushchair belonging to the homeless man
Who serenades you every morning
And claims he's Pavarotti's cousin,
In the city centre puddles
The birds bathe themselves in
All grouped up in a huddle
And in the corner
Of the nature photographer's photograph
That reveals two doggers dogging,
In the jealousy that arises

When you see two strangers snogging.
Exist in the cracks of life – in the parts
Awkward weeds grow through,
In the puzzle pieces that don't fit
That make life what it is
And soon enough you'll find yourself
Thrown down a wishing well, rich
Amongst all the coins at the bottom
Thrown without a doubt
With no intention ever
Of finding your way out.

The Facts

The fact is, is that the man who invented the high 5, only had 4 fingers. And the fact is there's more insects in one square mile of forest than there is humans in the world and the fact is the moon smells like fireworks. Speaking of the moon, Buzz Aldrin's mother's maiden name was Moon, and the fact is a phrase that goes 'it was written in the stars.' The fact is you can get 14 omelettes out of a single ostrich egg and the fact is giant snails hibernate half the year, so when you couldn't get out of bed in that one summer or one winter you needn't have worried because the facts were backing you up. Fact is, there's truth in the facts as a matter of fact that that's what makes them facts - and we love this truth. We love the fact that all sunflowers turned towards the sun or the fact that Beethoven was completely deaf when he composed his ninth symphony. Cause there's comfort in the truth and that's a fact can't argue with that. There's reassurance in the facts like how the word for Tory and Prime Minister both started out as insults or the fact that sea otters have a secret pocket in their armpits where they keep all their favourite stones or the fact that the first woman to ride a bike around the world learnt how to ride a bike the day before she left. These are the facts can't argue with that. The fact is the first northern presenter on the BBC was hired so that the Nazis could not impersonate the news. Interesting. The fact is it takes eight people to do an ultrasound on a python, and the fact is the Niagara Falls won't be here in 22,000 years but they're here now. The fact is we could get up and go see them if we wanted to. And the fact is there's facts we still don't have answers for, facts we don't know - we still don't have an answer for exactly why we kiss each other we don't know why human blood most resembles seawater – but we can wonder, oh can we wonder. And what we wonder can become our facts embedded in these things between our ears because the fact is we decide the facts about ourselves, we are our own composition - we choose our own facts don't be arguing with that. Because our names and our bodies and our worth - we make sense of it all we choose the fact we make the call. And speaking of the body, it takes 17 muscles to smile and 47 to frown and if your blood vessels were unfurled, they'd stretch around the whole of the world. And the fact is spiders have transparent blood and the fact is a whale's heart beats 9 times a minute and the fact is when your heart beats at what feels like 1000 times a minute listen - you're not dying.

It's just that the thing between our ears, it can reach out to the rest of the body and set things aflame, make it feel as though your chest is in this tightest of a cage and that's OK. Fact is it happens to me every other bloody day.

The fact is it might happen to you too and if it does the fact is we can talk about that so let's talk. Let's exchange our ways of keeping those things at bay because the fact is things get stuck. And the fact is when things get stuck it's the hardest thing to get them unstuck - take for example the list of things that have been found stuck in humans rectums including but not limited to a whiskey bottle, a spray can, a teacup, 5 carrots, a cucumber (naturally), a shampoo bottle accompanied by a bar of soap, two Vaseline jars, an 18 inch umbrella handle, a frozen pigs tail, a live eel, a Buzz Lightyear toy, a 1/2 full tobacco pouch, concrete mix, a peanut butter jar, an axe handle and five Tangerines at once. Cause things get stuck. Really stuck.

OK one more fact: and this is true, I promise you. Scientists have found that if you're stuck at the bottom of a well - I mean at the bottom in the muddy water – the fact is if you look up you can see the stars in the daytime. And that's a beautiful fact. And the fact is: the metaphor is obvious, but the fact is I'm going to use it anyway and say the fact is I was once going to choose to not be here anymore.

The fact is I couldn't think about anything else.

The fact is I still don't know why. But the other fact is I gave it time, and the fact is I took the steps and the fact is I began to undo it.

The fact is I chose to stay. The fact is you can too. And the fact is your prefrontal cortex developing at age 25 does not mean it's the end of your life. The fact is I chose to stay. The fact is you did too. The fact is that for the first 2 billion years the earth had no life on it in any way. The fact is I chose to stay. The fact is you can too, I promise you.

And those are the facts. Can't argue with that.

Scan this QR code to hear a live performance
of 'The Facts' with
Blue Ruth at Tell It To The Music, Birmingham
26.02.23

Kiss me, Birmingham

For mom and dad, because there has to be at least one.

Kiss me Birmingham, on a Missing Monday
During the climax of 'Young Hearts Run Free'
Kiss me in Snobs on a Wednesday,
Where I called my parents to come out to them as
'Half Gay'
Kiss me in Cannon Hill Park
On a pedalo swan we've commandeered
We can neck off in the underpass at Five Ways
And get lost in the Ikon
We can do tongues under the Digbeth lights
To the sweet sounds of whitewashed jazz
Or pretend a poem was about us at a Selly Oak open mic
Kiss me anywhere Birmingham
This place is a city of mirrors
Ten storeys high,
There'll be thousands of us
Kiss me at Maccies-on-the-Ramp at 2am
Kiss me after a Balti from Akram's down the road
Taste our many spices
Kiss me in Bournville by the open factory windows
Smell the chocolate in the air
Kiss me in Stirchley,
We'll do ourselves up and get gentrified, baby
We'll be brand spanking new
I'll go down on you down the row of houses I grew up along
Connected by their walls
And the music
And the conversations, melded through them
Connected by the bins put out and
The food passed over the fences

Kiss me in the park I went to after school
Where my laughter was spent like a debt
Kiss me in the place I first kissed a boy
Behind the bins in year ten
Where I first lit a cigarette
The same day, I'll have you know
Kiss me when the fog rolls through the city
And the skyscrapers linger, as if in a dream
And we can be lost, or so it seems
Kiss me, Birmingham
This place is a city of mirrors
Twenty storeys high
Kiss me on Ladypool Road
Kiss me by the roadworks so it never has to end
Kiss me with the accent I tried to lose out of a given shame
But never leaves
Kiss me by the old Ford Motors factory
Where me' Grandad lost his thumb
Kiss me on the canals in the
Lovely
Dirty
Green reflection
Kiss me on the balcony of Nightingales'
On any corner of Broad Street
Kiss me by the Hare and Hounds
To the echo of Ruby Turner, or Ozzy
Kiss me in the best bookshop in Birmingham
(Oxfam, Kings Heath)
Where I first found Benjamin Zephaniah and
Found my city in a lyric
Kiss me in the pissed in corners of Digbeth
By the graffiti
Oh, the artists that come out of this city
Poets, painters, singers, writers, anarchists of the time
They dot Birmingham like the stars they are

Birmingham, kiss me
On these streets I have run down my whole life
And still do now
And I know you're not perfect, but neither are we
The thousands of us, reflected in you
Because, Birmingham
Other than me' Mum and Dad
You,
You were the first thing I ever knew
On a cold night in April, 1998
Driven from the QE to Cotteridge
Your lights were the ones that passed by me in silent parade
And I was told it was snowing, in April
And I'm told this is exactly when my wonder and my love for you,
Birmingham,
Began.

ACKNOWLEDGEMENTS

Thank you to those talented individuals in the Birmingham poetry scene who shaped me, pushed me and kept me going. I will surely miss out some names here, but I would be nowhere without the following people: Mads, Ray, Zaki, Ayan, Jas, Casey, Scarlett, Lexia, Mickey, Paul Stringer, Nathan, Cory, Rick, Ben, Sarah, Ned, Peri, Thea, Dev, Ben, Memory, Josh, Erin, Eden, Leo, Leos dad, Vato, Amy, Ryan, Han, Aayushi, Mehdi, Keara, Steph, Strawbs, Beth, Hester, Hayley, Stuart, Liza, Nafeesa, Spitfiah, Ken, Liz Berry, Julie, Andy, Olive, Clemmie, Lee, Ken, Samiir, Kamil, Ilaf, Ade, Liv, Jack and Evie.

Thank you in particular to Scarlett Ward, who encouraged me to write poetry in the first place.

Thank you to the poets who I have had the absolute pleasure of meeting and getting to know along the way – Aish & Cal, Isabella Dorta, Danny Mash, Caitlyn O'Ryan, Joelle Taylor, Kandace Siobhan Walker, Sanah Ahsan, Harry Baker, Emmet O'Brien, Vanessa Kisuule, Sam J Grudgings, Malaika Kegode, Biz & Kate Ireland.

Thank you to Anong, Sadie & Jenny. You made a freezing house feel warm.

Thank you to Edie, Jim, Nikki and Tim. And Terza.

Thank you to Catherine and Claire of The Heath Bookshop for believing in me, being my mates and putting me on the Hare & Hounds stage in fishnets.

Thank you to all the bookshops in Brum, for your stock and for your love. Clive and Maria at Voce Books. Alison, Abi and the team at The Oxfam Bookshop, Kings Heath. Jenny from the Bear Bookshop. To my tiny family during my time at The Bookshop on The Green – Peri, Sarah and Doug. Thank you to The Poetry Bookshop in my home away from home, Hay on Wye.

Thank you to a ragtag bunch who helped me greatly along my way: Philip Holyman, Tracy King, Rafe Offer, Sam Straughn, Michael, Brett, Maya, Sian, Emily J Helen, Dan Lockheart, Craig Charles, Birmingham Tree People, William Gao, Olivia Hardy, Emy.

Thank you to my best mate Mads. For everything. As I told you, you make me feel okay with the passing of time. I can't wait to grow old together, you prick.

Thank you to that second family of mine that is my friends. To Mads, Izzy, Hannah, Ellie, Charlie Figg, Sarah, Mr Ray, Bill, Michael, Mia and Carrie. I love you.

Thank you to all you beautiful bastards who ever came to Overcoat Poetry. What fun we have. I hope by the time you're reading this we're still starting late, drinking too much wine and hearing the best poetry Brum has to offer.

Thank you, Tatyana.

Thank you to Katy Hawkins.

Thank you to my hairdresser Lydia, for the curls on my head are half the reason people know who I am.

Thank you to Emma Woolf and everyone else involved with the haven that is Cotteridge Park.

Thank you to Kafenion in Bournville.

Thank you to the wonderful team down at The Roundhouse.

Thank you to Adrian and my lovely Platform cohort from the Hay Festival 2024. I wish I could re-live those few days.

Thank you to Stuart at VERVE, for letting me be a diva about this book.

Thank you to anyone who has ever asked me for a poem during Poetry on Demand.

Thank you to Benjamin Zephaniahs family, in particular Minnie and David.

'Thank you to Evie for all your love and support.

Thank you to Ms Ledwidge for being that one teacher that changes everything.

Thank you to Codie, for everything.

Thank you to Roxanna for being the first person to read my poems when I was sticking them up on walls and trees, trying to find my voice again.

Thank you to the man in high-vis who walked me back across the bridge that day. I wish I knew your name.

Thank you Birmingham.

Thank you to my family – the mad bunch on the Priestley side and the even madder bunch on the Taylor side. Thank you especially to Becca, Lee and Dawn for believing in my work.

Thank you to my brother Aaron, for being my opposite and loving me anyway.

Thank you to my parents. I love you both more than I can say. And no, I won't get a proper job.

Thank you to my beloved nan and best friend, Pat – you taught me what a friend is.

And thank you! Yes, you. Lovely little you. You're great. Cheers for reading. Have a nice life. And remember – the best part hasn't even happened yet. You've missed nothing. I can't wait for it to happen. Let me know how it is.

All my love,

Bradley x

WRITE YOUR OWN DOOMSCROLLING THROUGH
INSTAGRAM POEM HERE:

ABOUT VERVE POETRY PRESS

Verve Poetry Press is a prize-winning press that focused initially on meeting a local need in Birmingham - a need for the vibrant poetry scene here in Brum to find a way to present itself to the poetry world via publication. Co-founded by Stuart Bartholomew and Amerah Saleh, it now publishes poets from all corners of the UK - poets that speak to the city's varied and energetic qualities and will contribute to its many poetic stories.

Added to this is a colourful pamphlet series, many featuring poets who have performed at our sister festival - and a poetry show series which captures the magic of longer poetry performance pieces by festival alumni such as Polarbear, Suhaiymah Manzoor-Khan and Imogen Stirling.

The press has been voted Most Innovative Publisher at the Saboteur Awards, and has won the Publisher's Award for Poetry Pamphlets at the Michael Marks Awards.

Like the festival, we strive to think about poetry in inclusive ways and embrace the multiplicity of approaches towards this glorious art.

www.vervepoetrypress.com
@VervePoetryPres
mail@vervepoetrypress.com